ROYAL COURT

The Royal Court Theatre presents

PRIMETIME

PRIMETIME was first performed at the Royal Court Jerwood Theatre Downstairs, Sloane Square, on Friday 19th July 2013 as part of the Kids Court Festival.

This production of PRIMETIME was first performed in the Jerwood Theatre Upstairs, Sloane Square, on Wednesday 28th May 2014.

PRIMETIME is a series of short plays written by playwrights who were at the time eight- to eleven-year-olds. They were developed during the Young Writers' Festival and Peckham Young Playwrights in 2012 with the help of Royal Court playwrights Nick Payne and Rachel De-lahay. The plays were performed in the Jerwood Theatre Downstairs in 2013 as part of a festival called Kids Court where children took over the theatre. A selection of the plays were then performed for the Royal Court PRIMETIME Schools Tour in London primary schools in 2014.

THE WRITERS

Temidayo Abayomi-Joseph, 9
Florence Adrian, 9
Jose Luis Aquino-Mejia, 9
Joseph Burke-Gaffney, 8
Naseem Charrat, 11
Ruby David-Pimlott, 10
Anya Davies, 9
Lucas Ferrar, 8
Jack Franco, 11
Isabelle Kennedy-Grimes, 9
Eva Kerslake-Blue, 8
Sultan Odukoya, 10

PRIMETIME KIDS COURT FESTIVAL 2013 CAST

Imgoen Doel
Christine Entwistle
Rebecca Humphries
James Marlowe
Sam Swann
Mark Weinman

The Young Writers' Festival development phase of PRIMETIME in 2011-12 was originally funded by John Lyon's Charity.

PRIMETIME SCHOOLS TOUR 2014

Cast in alphabetical order
Jason Barnett
Theo Cowan
Christine Entwisle
Sam Swann
Danielle Vitalis

Director **Ned Bennett**
Designer **Fly Davis**
Composer & Sound Designer **Giles Thomas**
Associate Composer & Sound Designer **Dom James**
Movement Director **Lucy Cullingford**
Casting Director **Lotte Hines**
Assistant Director **Debbie Hannan**
Education Associate **Lynne Gagliano**
Education Apprentice **Maia Clarke**
Production Manager **Niall Black**
Producer **Holly Gladwell**
Stage Managers **Fiona Kennedy & Andrew Beckett**
Costume Supervisor **Jessica Knight**
Workshop Co-ordinator **Katherine Gill**
Additional Music Composed by **Dom James**

The 2014 PRIMETIME Schools Tour has received additional support from
Dr Kate Best, John McNeil, Rob & Siri Cope and Glenn & Phyllida Earle.

The Royal Court and Stage Management wish to thank the following for their help
with this production: Marec Joyce, George Cook, Heather Cryan, Ruth Stringer,
Zoe Hurwitz, Chloe Lamford, Grape Street.

THE COMPANY

JASON BARNETT (Ensemble)

FOR THE ROYAL COURT: Friday Night Sex, The Victorian in the Wall, The Girlfriend Experience.

OTHER THEATRE INCLUDES: Emil & the Detectives, War Horse, Amato Saltone (National); About a Boy (Young Vic/tour); Mogadishu (Royal Exchange, Manchester); The Winter's Tale, Pericles, Days of Significance (RSC); The Fixer (Almeida); Cruisin' (Bush); I Am Mediocre (BAC); John Dryden's Tempest (Globe); The 1966 World Cup Final (BAC/tour).

TELEVISION INCLUDES: Bad Education, Phoneshop, The Javone Prince Show, Stagedoor Johnnies, Hotel Trubble, The Legend of Dick & Dom, The Bill, Doctors, Extras, The Vivien Vyle Show, Coming of Age, Dead Ringers, Dream Team, Little Britain.

FILM INCLUDES: Cinderella, Superbob, London Road, One Man & His Dog.

Jason is an associate actor with Synergy Theatre Project and a producer with Graft Films.

NED BENNETT (Director)

FOR THE ROYAL COURT: Pigeons (Schools tour), Lost in Theatre, Primetime.

AS ASSISTANT DIRECTOR, FOR THE ROYAL COURT: Pigeons, Death Tax, The President Has Come To See You, Collaboration, No Quarter, Narrative, If You Don't Let Us Sleep We Won't Let You Dream, The Ritual Slaughter of Gorge Mastromas.

AS DIRECTOR, THEATRE INCLUDES: Pomona (RWCMD/Gate); Superior Donuts (Southwark Playhouse); Mercury Fur (Old Red Lion/Trafalgar Studios); Mr Noodles (Royal Exchange, Manchester); Blue Rabbits (Templeworks); Excellent Choice (Old Vic Tunnels); A Butcher of Distinction (King's Head); Edmond (Theatre Royal, Haymarket); Smartcard (Shunt Vaults); Selling Clive (Lost).

AS ASSISTANT DIRECTOR, THEATRE INCLUDES: Of Mice & Men (Watermill); A Letter to England (Finborough); Odette (Bridewell); Vent (Contact).

THEO COWAN (Ensemble)

THEATRE INCLUDES: Lord of the Flies (Regent's Park Open Air); A Touch of the Sun, Tamburlaine (Bristol Old Vic).

TELEVISION INCLUDES: Sparticle Mystery, Caught in the Web, Doctors.

FLY DAVIS (Designer)

AS DESIGNER, FOR THE ROYAL COURT: Pigeons, Collaboration, Primetime.

AS ASSOCIATE DESIGNER, FOR THE ROYAL COURT: Open Court Season, No Quarter, Disconnect.

AS DESIGNER, THEATRE INCLUDES: I'd Rather Goya Robbed Me of My Sleep Than Some Other Arsehole (Gate); Hunger for Trade (Royal Exchange, Manchester); Superior Donuts (Southwark Playhouse); Khadija is 18, Almost Near, The Man (Finborough); What the Animals Say (Greyscale); The Great British Country Fête (Bush/UK tour); England Street (Oxford Playhouse); Life Support (Theatre Royal York); Woyzeck (Omnibus); Change (Arcola); 'Ave It (Old Vic Tunnels); CHAVS (Lyric Hammersmith); The Wonderful World of Dissocia, Deathwatch, The White Guard (Drama Centre).

AS ASSOCIATE DESIGNER, THEATRE INCLUDES: Playhouse Presents (Sky Arts), A Play A Pie & A Pint (Paines Plough), The Whisky Taster (Bush).

MUSIC VIDEOS INCLUDE: McFly's Love is Easy.

CHRISTINE ENTWISLE (Ensemble)

FOR THE ROYAL COURT: Primetime, Narrative, The Wonderful World of Dissocia (& National tour/Edinburgh International Festival).

OTHER THEATRE INCLUDES: Billy the Girl (Clean Break/Soho); As You Like It, The Comedy of Errors, Romeo & Juliet, Morte D'Athur (RSC); Six Characters in Search of an Author (Gielgud/Headlong/Chichester Festival); Half Life (National Theatre of Scotland); C'est Vauxhall! (Barbican); Genetics for Blondes (Soho); The Wedding (Southwark Playhouse/National tour); Vassa (Almeida/The Albery); A Family Affair (Clwyd); Wonderhorse (Edinburgh International Festival/ICA/BAC); Edward Gant's Amazing Feats of Loneliness (Theatre Royal Plymouth); I Am Dandy (Purcell Rooms/BAC); Ubu Kunst, Missing Jesus (Young Vic);

Paper Walls (Scarlet/Assembly Rooms/Purcell Rooms); Fine (Young Vic/Edinburgh International Festival); People Shows 100-103 (International tour).

TELEVISION INCLUDES: Attachments, Holby City, Mothers & Daughters, At Dawning, A&E, Where the Heart Is, Dalziel & Pascoe, Storm Damage, Deeper Still.

RADIO INCLUDES: Heredity.

DEBBIE HANNAN (Assistant Director)

AS DIRECTOR, FOR THE ROYAL COURT: Peckham: The Soap Opera (co-director).

AS ASSISTANT DIRECTOR, FOR THE ROYAL COURT: Birdland, The Mistress Contract.

AS DIRECTOR, OTHER THEATRE INCLUDES: Notes from the Underground (Citizens); Panorama, Roses Are Dead, You Cannot Call it Love (Arches); Yellow Pears (Swept Up); liberty, equality, fraternity (Tron/Traverse); Grimm Tales, Nights at the Circus (Paradok).

AS ASSISTANT DIRECTOR, THEATRE INCLUDES: A Doll's House, Enquirer (National Theatre of Scotland/Lyceum); The Maids, Beauty & the Beast (Citizens); Kurt Weill: Double Bill (Scottish Opera); War of the Roses Trilogy (Bard in the Botanics); Hamlet (Globe Education).

Debbie is Trainee Director at the Royal Court.

DOM JAMES (Associate Composer & Sound Designer)

AS COMPOSER, THEATRE INCLUDES: Imaginarium (Village Underground); The Pilgrim's Progress (St James' Muswell Hill); Remix (BAC); Yvonne (Hoxton Hall).

AS MUSIC ASSISTANT, THEATRE INCLUDES: Cat in the Hat (National).

TELEVISION INCLUDES: Come Dine With Me, Facejacker, A Child's Christmas in Wales (additional music), Lifeline (additional music).

FILM INCLUDES: Passing By, The Life & Death of 9413 A Hollywood Extra, Intel Ultrabook Revolution, Burning Man & the Meaning of Life, Just Because You're Paranoid.

MUSIC VIDEOS INCLUDE: Tinie Tempah's Wonderman.

Working primarily from his studio in South London, Dom composes across many genres including TV, film, theatre, commercials and even theme park rides. He is a specialist in the New Orleans clarinet style and performs regularly with his jazz band The Dixie Ticklers.

SAM SWANN (Ensemble)

FOR THE ROYAL COURT: Primetime.

OTHER THEATRE INCLUDES: Wendy & Peter (RSC); A Winter's Tale (Unicorn); Dr Korczak's Example (Unicorn/Royal Exchange, Manchester); Mercury Fur (Trafalgar Studios); Anne & Zef (Salibury Playhouse); The Kitchen, Greenland (National); A Butcher of Distinction (Cock Tavern/King's Head); Powder Monkey (Royal Exchange, Manchester); The Exclusion Zone (Southwark Playhouse); Dunsinane (Hampstead/RSC); Waiting for Godot (Birmingham Library).

TELEVISION INCLUDES: Privates, Doctors, Navid & Johnny, Boom!

FILM INCLUDES: Latvia, The Owl & the Pussycat, The Listener, O Romeo Romeo, What Light?.

RADIO INCLUDES: The Interrogation, Obey the Wave, The Trenches Trip, The Second Mr Bailey.

GILES THOMAS (Composer & Sound Designer)

FOR THE ROYAL COURT: Talk Show, Untitled Matriarch Play (or Seven Sisters), Collaboration, Mint, Death Tax, The President Has Come to See You, Shoot/Get Treasure/Repeat (Gate/National/Out of Joint/Paines Plough).

AS COMPOSER/SOUND DESIGNER: Superior Donuts (Southwark); Henry V (West End); Take A Deep Breath & Breathe, The Street (Oval House); Stop Kiss (Leicester Square); Three Men In a Boat (Original Theatre Company); King John (Unity); It's About Time (nabokov); House of Agnes (Paines Plough).

AS MUSIC PRODUCER: An Appointment with the Wickerman (National Theatre of Scotland).

Giles trained at the Liverpool Institute of Performing Arts. He also writes for TV, Film and Video Games and is one of the co-founders of the composition company Contour Chromatic.

DANIELLE VITALIS (Ensemble)

THEATRE INCLUDES: Holloway Jones (Synergy); Dream Pill (Clean Break/Underbelly); Dancing Bears (Clean Break/Latitude); Every Coin (Synergy/Soho); Re-Charged, Charged – Dream Pill, Charged – Dancing Bears (Clean Break/Soho); White Something (Arcola); Bugsy Malone (Stratford Circus); Demon Juice (Stratford Circus/Royal Opera House).

TELEVISION INCLUDES: In the Flesh, Youngers, The Riots: In Their Own Words, L8R, La Boheme.

FILM INCLUDES: Honeytrap, Attack the Block.

RADIO INCLUDES: What Would Elizabeth Bennett Do?, Burning Up, The Burning Times.

THE ENGLISH STAGE COMPANY
AT THE ROYAL COURT THEATRE

The Royal Court is the writers' theatre. It is a leading force in world theatre, finding writers and producing new plays that are original and contemporary. The Royal Court strives to be at the centre of civic, political, domestic and international life, giving writers a home to tackle big ideas and world events and tell great stories.

photo: Stephen Cummiskey

The Royal Court commissions and develops an extraordinary quantity of new work, reading over 3000 scripts a year and annually producing around 14 world or UK premieres in its two auditoria at Sloane Square in London. Over 200,000 people visit the Royal Court each year and many thousands more see our work elsewhere through transfers to the West End and New York, national and international tours, residencies across London and site-specific work, including recent Theatre Local Seasons in Peckham, King's Cross and Haggerston.

The Royal Court's extensive development activity encompasses a diverse range of writers and artists and includes an ongoing programme of writers' attachments, readings, workshops and playwriting groups. Twenty years of pioneering work around the world means the Royal Court has relationships with writers on every continent.

The Royal Court opens its doors to radical thinking and provocative discussion, and to the unheard voices and free thinkers that, through their writing, change our way of seeing.

"With its groundbreaking premieres and crusading artistic directors, the Royal Court has long enjoyed a reputation as one of our most daring, seat-of-its-pants theatres." The Times

"The most important theatre in Europe." New York Times

Within the past sixty years, John Osborne, Arnold Wesker and Howard Brenton have all started their careers at the Court. Many others, including Caryl Churchill, Mark Ravenhill and Sarah Kane have followed. More recently, the theatre has found and fostered new writers such as Polly Stenham, Mike Bartlett, Bola Agbaje, Nick Payne and Rachel De-lahay and produced many iconic plays from Laura Wade's *Posh* to Bruce Norris' *Clybourne Park* and Jez Butterworth's *Jerusalem*. Royal Court plays from every decade are now performed on stage and taught in classrooms across the globe.

Supported by
ARTS COUNCIL
ENGLAND

ROYAL COURT SUPPORTERS

The Royal Court has significant and longstanding relationships with many organisations and individuals who provide vital support. It is this support that makes possible its unique playwriting and audience development programmes.

Coutts supports Innovation at the Royal Court. The Genesis Foundation supports the Royal Court's work with International Playwrights. Theatre Local is sponsored by Bloomberg. AlixPartners support The Big Idea at the Royal Court. The Jerwood Charitable Foundation supports emerging writers through the Jerwood New Playwrights series. The Andrew Lloyd Webber Foundation supports the Royal Court's Studio, which aims to seek out, nurture and support emerging playwrights. The Pinter Commission is given annually by his widow, Lady Antonia Fraser, to support a new commission at the Royal Court.

PUBLIC FUNDING
Arts Council England, London
British Council

CHARITABLE DONATIONS
Martin Bowley Charitable Trust
Cowley Charitable Trust
The Dorset Foundation
The Eranda Foundation
Genesis Foundation
The Golden Bottle Trust
The Haberdashers' Company
The Idlewild Trust
Jerwood Charitable Foundation
Marina Kleinwort Trust
The Andrew Lloyd Webber Foundation
John Lyon's Charity
Clare McIntyre's Bursary
The Andrew W. Mellon Foundation
The David & Elaine Potter Foundation
Rose Foundation
Royal Victoria Hall Foundation
The Sackler Trust
The Sobell Foundation
John Thaw Foundation
The Vandervell Foundation
Sir Siegmund Warburg's Voluntary Settlement
The Garfield Weston Foundation
The Wolfson Foundation

CORPORATE SUPPORTERS & SPONSORS
AKA
Alix Partners
American Airlines
Aqua Financial Solutions Ltd
BBC
Bloomberg

Café Colbert
Coutts
Fever-Tree
Gedye & Sons
Kudos Film & Television
MAC
Moët & Chandon
Quintessentially Vodka
Smythson of Bond Street
White Light Ltd

BUSINESS ASSOCIATES, MEMBERS & BENEFACTORS
Annoushka
Auerbach & Steele Opticians
Bank of America Merrill Lynch
Byfield Consultancy
Capital MSL
Cream
Lazard
Vanity Fair
Waterman Group

DEVELOPMENT ADVOCATES
Elizabeth Bandeen
Anthony Burton CBE
Piers Butler
Sindy Caplan
Sarah Chappatte
Cas Donald (Vice Chair)
Celeste Fenichel
Piers Gibson
Emma Marsh (Chair)
Deborah Shaw Marquardt (Vice Chair)
Tom Siebens
Sian Westerman
Daniel Winterfeldt

Supported by
ARTS COUNCIL ENGLAND

Innovation Partner

Make a Donation

By making a donation to the Royal Court you can help us to respond to new and established playwrights, and supply them with the time, resources and environment to follow their imagination and exceed their potential.

Help us to make the Royal Court the renowned international success that it is.

To make a donation to the Royal Court, please:
Call Anna Sampson on 020 7565 5049
Email annasampson@royalcourttheatre.com
Visit royalcourttheatre.com/support-us/make-a-donation

Thank you in advance for supporting our work and changing theatre forever.

www.royalcourttheatre.com

The English Stage Company at the Royal Court Theatre is a registered charity (No. 231242).

Photo: John Haynes

PRIMETIME

PRIMETIME

Short plays by primary school
children aged 8-11

EVA KERSLAKE-BLUE

JACK FRANCO

JOSEPH BURKE-GAFFNEY

ISABELLE KENNEDY-GRIMES

JOSE LUIS AQUINO-MEJIA

NASEEM CHARRAT

ANYA DAVIES

FLORENCE ADRIAN

TEMIDAYO ABAYOMI-JOSEPH

LUCAS FERRAR

RUBY DAVID-PIMLOTT

SULTAN ODUKOYA

OBERON BOOKS
LONDON

WWW.OBERONBOOKS.COM

First published in 2014 by Oberon Books Ltd

521 Caledonian Road, London N7 9RH

Tel: +44 (0) 20 7607 3637 / Fax: +44 (0) 20 7607 3629

e-mail: info@oberonbooks.com

www.oberonbooks.com

PB ISBN: 978-1-78319-150-5

E ISBN: 978-1-78319-649-4

The following scripts are published exactly as written by the playwrights, aged 8–11

Cat or what?

BY EVA KERSLAKE-BLUE

Cast

ENID APPLE-BLACK

MOLLY PEAR-BROWN

JESSIE LEMON-PINK

SCENE ONE

A dark room, you can only just see the outline of a wooden desk and chair in the corner. There is the sound of a match being struck.

ENID: *(ENID is leaning over the desk, lighting a candle. You can just see her long dark hair streaming over her face like a pitch-black waterfall. She sits down at her desk and starts to write her diary in concentration. You can hear the scratch of her pen on the paper. Her voice is heard narrating what she writes echoing out her thoughts from above. Her voice is dreamy, like she is hypnotised.)*

I am Enid Apple-Black and I am turning into a cat.

(ENID stops, holds up her hand in front of her eyes, turns it back and forth, sighs, and starts writing again.)

The first thing that I noticed was that I was drawn like a magnet to the delicious fish counter in Tesco…mmm…

(A spotlight appears on stage, lighting up a gigantic brightly coloured fish, slowly flipping over and over.)

(Another spotlight appears behind the first one, showing ENID looking at her face in a mirror.)

The second thing that I noticed was that my hair suddenly grew sleek and shiny. Thick too. It reminded me of something. Something not human but something I had touched before.

(The spot-lit ENID mimes brushing her hair and starts touching her face.)

The third thing was that sharp stubs started to appear on my face. What could they be? I thought. Was I turning into a man? An old lady? A shiver went down my spine as I touched them.

(The spotlights all go out.)

The *fourth* thing that I noticed was really weird. I was looking at my stubby cheeks when I noticed my eyes! One of them had a diamond-shaped pupil while the other one looked the same as normal.

(Diamond-shaped lights flicker across the stage.)

When I went to school, I tried hard to hide all the changes. I had never really had any friends and longed to be the most popular girl in the class like Jessie Lemon-Pink. *Everybody* loves Jessie Lemon-Pink, the girl who gets *all* the attention. Plus I really don't want to be like Molly Pear-Brown who is the most shy and unpopular girl in the class, if not the whole school!

(JESSIE LEMON-PINK dances across the stage in a baby pink, short and flouncy ballet tutu, her long flowing strawberry blond hair piled up in a bun on top of her head. Behind her, MOLLY PEAR-BROWN scuttles along, not taking her eyes off the ground.)

I wore long-sleeved black tops to hide my hairy arms and thick leggings to hide my hairy legs and a hoody pulled low to hide my weird eyes.

One day, though, I couldn't hide my transformation any longer.

(Sound of a crack of thunder and dramatic music.)

It was so hot that I went to school without my disguise. I just forgot! It was like a nightmare. Everybody stared. Molly Pear-Brown burst into tears and Jessie Lemon-Pink laughed…

(MOLLY PEAR-BROWN and JESSIE LEMON-PINK run onto the stage, one crying, the other laughing. ENID comes out from behind the desk and walks between them. She speaks directly to the audience.)

Before I knew what was happening, I sank onto all fours, hissed and stuck out my claws.

(ENID does that, looking really vicious.)

(The stage goes black and you can only hear ENID's voice.)

Since then I have been living in a place that I named Nowhere.

SCENE TWO

JESSIE LEMON-PINK is standing in an empty playground, dressed entirely in pink, speaking into a pink mobile phone.

JESSIE: Oh, for God's sake, won't you just get over here? I've been waiting for ages! *(Listens, boredly.)* Okay, okay, just hurry up!

(JESSIE snaps the phone shut and starts examining her nails and grooming her head.)

(In the background ENID appears, dressed up, looking as glam as a celebrity and singing a weird song.)

ENID: *(ENID slinks in, singing in a low growly voice.)*

I sank onto all fours
I stuck out my sharp new claws
Nobody mess with me
You'll see how mean I can be

(JESSIE doesn't seem to hear her and continues grooming her nails. ENID slinks up and stands behind JESSIE.)

Meow.

JESSIE: *(Turns and ruffles up ENID's long sleek and shiny hair.)*

You're here at last, you naughty puss.

(ENID purrs and nuzzles her head under JESSIE's hand.)

I've got so much to tell you! You'll never guess what I did to Alice Kiwi-White!

ENID: Meow? Meow?

JESSIE: It was hilarious! I flushed her school skirt down the toilet after swimming and she had to spend the afternoon with her towel wrapped round her bum!

ENID: Meeeoooouuuwww! Meow! Meow! *(Like cackling laughter.)*

JESSIE: And you know that big fat blob, Susan Banana-Grey?

ENID: Meow?

JESSIE: I put salt in her ice cream and she couldn't eat it and she burst into tears right in front of everyone in the lunch hall. I sat opposite her and made sure she could see me lapping up my ice cream.

ENID: Meow! *(Like laughing.)*

(JESSIE starts rubbing ENID's head and they both laugh horribly.)

(In the background behind them, MOLLY PEAR-BROWN edges silently along hoping that they won't see her. But JESSIE turns and spots her.)

JESSIE: Well, well. If it isn't that little wimpy Molly, eh? What are you doing, you sneaky little rat?

(MOLLY stands frozen to the spot as JESSIE and ENID creep closer to her, their hands outstretched like cat's paws with long claws. JESSIE starts to bat MOLLY over the head while laughing and hissing.)

ENID: *(Steps back to the side.)*

Meow. *(Sad.)*

(MOLLY crouches on the ground as JESSIE continues to bat at her. She puts her hands over her head. ENID walks to the front and stands looking out at the audience, her head on one side, confused.)

SCENE THREE

MOLLY PEAR-BROWN is in the deserted playground, sitting on the floor, her head hanging down.

MOLLY: I'm so sick of this. Why is everyone so mean?

(She sobs.)

(ENID slinks onto the stage, looking shy. MOLLY doesn't see her until she nuzzles up under MOLLY's hand.)

ENID: Meow?

(MOLLY pushes her off.)

MOLLY: What do *you* want? You...you...you freak!

ENID: Meow!

(She starts to roll on the floor and do things to make herself look cute like cats do.)

MOLLY: Get away from me you mangy cat! You are so weird!

ENID: *(Sits up, looks puzzled.)*

Meow?

(From the other side, JESSIE appears and walks straight up to ENID, grabs her by the scruff of her neck.)

JESSIE: So you want to be friends with her, do you? You were supposed to be *my* pet. You make me sick.

(She turns to MOLLY and gives a sugary sweet smile.)

Hi Molly, how are you? I *love* your coat!

MOLLY: *(Looks pleased.)*

Thanks Jessie. My mum got it from Ebay...I mean, from John Lewis.

JESSIE: *(Smiles sneakily, pushes ENID away with her foot and links her arm through MOLLY's.)*

Fancy coming to hang out with me for a while?

MOLLY: *(Looks delighted, jumps up and down, then stops and tries to look cool.)*

Yes, sure. Let's go!

(MOLLY and JESSIE link arms and walk off together chatting and laughing. ENID is left on the floor. She picks herself up, licks her paws, then walks to the front of the stage again, with the same confused expression like before.)

SCENE FOUR

JESSIE is sitting alone in the same playground as before. She looks slightly untidy, her hair is falling down and she is fiddling with her mobile phone.

JESSIE: I'm sick of this phone. It must be broken. Otherwise she would have called! I know she would. She's my best friend!

(JESSIE puts her head in her hands and starts sobbing. To the side, ENID struts in talking on her mobile phone.)

ENID: Miouw. Miouw. Miouw-miouw-miouw.

(ENID sees JESSIE and comes over. JESSIE smiles and falls to her knees and starts kissing ENID's feet.)

JESSIE: Oh Enid, you look wonderful. I've missed you so much! Where have you been? Do you still love me? Do you? Say you do!

ENID: *(Yawns and kicks JESSIE away.)*

Miouw. *(Bored.)*

(Suddenly ENID pounces and pushes her face close to JESSIE. JESSIE freezes.)

(From the other side, MOLLY walks in. She sees ENID and waves and bounces over.)

MOLLY: Enid! You look wonderful. I've missed you so much! Where have you been? Do you still love me? Do you? Say you do!

ENID: *(Yawns and pushes MOLLY away.)*

Miouw. *(Bored.)*

(Suddenly ENID pounces up to MOLLY and pushes her face close to MOLLY. MOLLY freezes.)

(ENID takes a mirror from her bag, looks at her reflection then freezes.)

(After a moment, ENID 'wakes up' and walks to the front and talks.)

I spy with my diamond eye something beginning with…
friends! It all begins with friends!

SCENE FIVE

(We return to the first scene where ENID enters the dark room and lights a candle and starts writing. Her voice narrates what she's writing like before.)

ENID: My name is Enid Apple-Black and I am *not* turning into a cat. It's no good being Nowhere. Nowhere is where you have no friends.

(The lights all come on. ENID sits up, stretches, then starts to clap and sing the 'ENID' song. From the other two sides, JESSIE and MOLLY come in, clapping too.)

Cat, cat, on a mat
How d'you get to be as mean as that?

Cat, cat, on a mat
How d'you get to be as mean as that?

Cat, cat, on a mat
How d'you get to be as mean as that?

Cat, cat, on a mat
How d'you get to be as mean as that?

Cat, cat, on a mat
How d'you get to be as mean as that?

(As she gets to the front of the stage, JESSIE and MOLLY are behind her like backing singers and they join in with the song, getting louder and louder until they finally all stop, freeze, then the lights go down.)

The End.

London, we have a problem

BY JACK FRANCO

Cast

TED HUTCHINS
boy of 12 years of age

SPENCER
factory worker, Battersea power station

MIKE
Ted's brother, 17 years of age, also a factory worker

SCENE 1

London, 1969.

TED: Evenin' Spencer.

SPENCER: Look who's here, my favourite little scoundrel.

TED: How's life in that killing machine?

SPENCER: A fair income as always, nothing more and nothing less.

MIKE: Thank God for that, Spencer me old moose!!!

SPENCER: 'ave you heard Mike, the first man on the moon today!!!

MIKE: Yes, we should celebrate!

TED: *(Under his breath.)* I guess they haven't heard yet, a nuclear alert in that very power station where Old Spencer works!

SPENCER: Blimey, Ted why didn't you tell us before, you could have killed us, but not in Battersea power station!!??

MIKE: Putting that to one side, how did you know anyway?

TED: Well you know, that old Grouch of a man, Old Bill?

MIKE: Yes, the one that sits on a rocking chair all day.

SPENCER: *(Interrupting.)* Never listen to that old bag!

TED: What the hell is that burning smell coming from the power station?

MIKE: *(Showing of his intellect proudly.)* Just a blown electrical fuse I believe but if I put some wires there, connect the blue with the red and put some oil and coal into the furnace it should be solved.

SFX: explosion sound.

SPENCER: I bet my life's earnings that you were going to cause a problem, Ted, don't listen to that crap Mike keeps banging on about, grab your stuff and start a-runnin'!!!

Shouts from outside, the characters not visible.

Crowd running Factory workers evacuating.

SCENE 2

On a country lane towards Aylesbury.

SPENCER: What the Flip did you have in mind, Mike?

MIKE: Well, all the other nuclear alerts have been blown fuses, so I assumed that this would be a fuse too.

SPENCER: Never trust common happenings and never assume things you have never experienced.

BEGGAR: *(Dressed in rags and sitting on a fence.)* Could you spare a pound for a cup of tea for a poor suffering chap like me.

MIKE: *(Sarcastically.)* Let me think… No.

SPENCER: What's your name old chap?

BEGGAR/STEVE: *(With an Irish accent.)* Oi be Steve from Oirland, sir.

TED: What are you doing here Mister Steve?

STEVE: Oi be running away from London after that nuclear disaster!

SPENCER: Right then Steve me old chap, you can come with our team of factory workers and a little young 'un.

STEVE: Oi thank 'ee so much.

MIKE: *(Under his breath.)* You can say that again.

STEVE: Oi thank 'ee so much.

TED: Let's get a move on you lazy old grouches.

SPENCER: Let's head to a pub, to drown our sorrows.

TED: I don't drink.

SPENCER: Let's have something to eat then.

TED: I ain't hungry!

SPENCER: Shut your noggin', we are having something to eat whether you like it or not.

SCENE 3

At the pub.

MIKE: Why don't we get a nice house round these parts and lead a good life.

STEVE: Oi agree with that oi do.

TED: Yes we can have a nice house and a nice job with a nice life in a nice country with a nice grey sky!

SPENCER: *(Coughing growing gradually louder.)* Yes – cough – we could do that – COUGH – if we save ourselves from that polluted water world we will!

MIKE: Why do you keep coughin', is something wrong?

SPENCER: I am all right.

STEVE: It don't look like it, it looks like you have bronchioloalveolar lung carcinoma.

TED: You can say that again!

STEVE: It looks like you have bronchioloalveolar lung carcinoma.

MIKE: Holy cow, you could die of this!!

SPENCER: *(Slaps MIKE.)* And that's for blasphemy!

TED: Quick let's take a cab and go to our old friend Doc Jasper.

CAB DRIVER: Where to?

MIKE: The suburban hospital in the middle of nowhere.

SCENE 4

The Suburban Hospital In The Middle Of Nowhere.

CAB DRIVER: £6.80.

MIKE: Come on, give us a discount, we needed to get to the hospital because our friend is dying, and now we won't have enough money for surgery; you must help us!

CAB DRIVER: Fine then, 5 quid.

MIKE: Thank you so much!!!

DOC JASPER: What seems to be the problem, Spencer?

STEVE: He has bronchioloalveolar lung carcinoma.

MIKE: *(He stops in the middle of the sentence at the dash.)* 'xactly he has tha – 'old on a minute who told you his diagnosis, you're not 'Doctor Steve' now are ya!

TED: Just give him a check up and surgery if he needs it, he is the only person that can care for me along with Mike!!

(Scene interrupted by a radio: 'it has just been known that Great Britain has declared war on Luxembourg, therefore all men above the age of 16 must report to the nearest police station or army base, this as you know is compulsory'… the radio fades away and the scene continues.)

TED: Now that Mike has to go to the army, Spencer is the only man who can care for me!!

NARRATION: *The operation on Spencer has failed and Spencer dies. Further on Mike has joined up in the army, he receives the Victoria Cross and returns home victorious. He then also dies of cancer.*

SCENE 5

SFX: ka boom.

Siren.

TED: Another nuclear explosion, grab your stuff and leg it!!!!!!!!!!!!

STEVE: Right let's get a move on!

TED: Back to London its our only hope!!!

STEVE: You're right, we need to get moving.

WAITER: The nearest route is in the tube station.

TED: Take us to Buckingham palace.

STEVE: What?

TED: We are getting jobs at the Queen's residence.

SCENE 6

The Buckingham Palace throne room.

TED: Your Majesty we would like a job as your advisors on environment events and happenings.

QUEEN: Perfect, you're just what I needed, someone who cares for my gardens and the trees of the world, you're hired, George your sacked!

TED: Steve now we have a job we can 'ave a proper lifestyle/

STEVE: 'Xactly.

TED: Now we have a perfect life and Spencer and Mike would love this too, they could get rid of nature killing machines.

STEVE: 2 Minutes' Silence for their deaths.

Two minutes go by.

STEVE: Thank'ee for watching.

RADIO: *(Muffled voices from outer space.)* London, we have a problem.

The End.

The Flying Boy

BY JOSEPH BURKE-GAFFNEY

SCENE 1

Inside a very normal, boring house.

MAX, aged 10, and his MUM are in a messy living room.

MAX: Mum, I'm bored.

MUM: OK Max… Why don't you do some planting in the garden?

MAX: *(In a bored way.)* All right then.

SCENE 2

In the garden (MAX starts digging with a trowel).

Suddenly he sees a sign sticking out of the earth. He digs a bit more to uncover it.

MAX: *(Holding up the sign and reading it.)* 'Learn to Fly…this way.' How weird – whichever way I hold this sign, it always points down here….oh! Wow! What's that? It's a kind of swirly whirlpool in the earth. Even weirder! And the sign is telling me to jump in…well I <u>would</u> like to fly. So, here goes…

(MAX holds his nose and jumps in.)

SCENE 3

In a beautiful garden with sand on the ground.

MAX: Wow! This is pretty strange. And weird. And beautiful. I wonder where I am.

(Enter a yellow long-nosed hippopotamus called Gary.)

GARY: So, you'd like to fly, huh? Well me too, but I'm afraid *(Shouts.)* WE DON'T HAVE ANY POTION!

MAX: Ok, but no need to shout. Er…who are you anyway, if you don't mind me asking?

GARY: I'm Gary, the yellow long-nosed hippo OF COURSE. Who are you?

MAX: I'm Max the normal-nosed human. And please don't shout.

GARY: *(Upset.)* I'm sorry. It's just that I'm sad that there's no potion left to make us fly.

MAX: What, you're a flying centre and you don't have any potion?

GARY: *(Sadly, hanging his long nose down.)* That's right. None at all.

MAX: Well why don't we go and find some?

GARY: Because we'd have to go to Russia and India to get the ingredients. And without the potion to make us fly, we can't fly there to get the ingredients for the potion. If you see what I mean.

MAX: But hold on a minute. I might have some magic I can help you with.

GARY: What magic?

MAX: The magic of teleporting. I've just collected some potion from near my home. I live in France. The potion makes you able to teleport. It's a potion for life. Once you've drunk the teleporting juice, the pot fills up again. It's so cool.

GARY: Ok Max, let's go!

MAX: Hold my hand and hold your nose!

(MAX and GARY hold hands and hold their noses then jump.)

SCENE 4

Outside a Russian palace.

(MAX and GARY are standing in an amazing square in front of a Russian palace.)

MAX: So here we are. What ingredient do we need for the flying potion, Gary?

GARY: We need a piece of a Russian palace.

MAX: Let's have a look around.

(MAX and GARY look around.)

(Enter RUSSIAN PRINCE.)

RUSSIAN PRINCE: *(Muttering.)* I love peas. I love peas so much…fresh green peas. If only I could have some peas.

GARY and MAX look at each other as if to say 'weird'.

MAX: Hi there. I'm Max. I just heard you say that you love peas. I've got some here in my pocket. I was going to plant them. Would you like them?

PRINCE: *(Excited.)* What! You have peas? I love peas. When my evil uncle killed my father seven years ago, he took our land just before harvest and I haven't had a pea since then.

MAX: *(Hands over peas.)* There you go.

PRINCE: Thank you so much. *(Eats the peas.)* Is there anything I can get you in return?

GARY: Well, actually. Is there any chance we could have a tiny piece of your palace to make a magic potion so we can fly?

PRINCE: You're very lucky. We're having building work done today. You can take a big chunk of the old palace.

(PRINCE hunts around and finds a piece of palace wall.)

PRINCE: Here you are.

GARY AND MAX: Thank you so much. Goodbye.

PRINCE: Goodbye my friends. Peas be with you!

(GARY and MAX hold hands, hold their noses and jump.)

SCENE 5

An Indian jungle. MAX and GARY are in the jungle.

MAX: Ok Gary, so what do we need from India?

GARY: A hair from the tail of a Indian monkey.

MAX: But where are we going to find a monk…?

(Enter a band of monkeys, one singing, one drumming and one playing guitar. They are also drinking cocktails. They are singing 'We love cocktails! We love cocktails!' Then slurping their drinks.)

MAX: Hi guys!

The DRUMMER MONKEY comes forward.

DRUMMER MONKEY: Hi! I love cocktails.

MAX: So we heard.

GARY: Would you by any chance like some of these mini umbrellas to put in your cocktails? *(MONKEYS come running up and take the umbrellas, dancing around with them.)*

DRUMMER MONKEY: Hey! Mini umbrellas! Cool, thanks!

MAX: Er…please could we have a tiny hair from your tails to help us make a magic potion.

DRUMMER MONKEY: Sure. Go ahead.

(MAX and GARY collect hairs from each of the three monkeys.)

MAX AND GARY: Thank you!

GARY: Now I can make the potion.

MAX: Excellent!

(GARY makes the potion, using his long nose to mix it up.

GARY hands a little bottle to MAX.)

GARY: Here – drink this!

(MAX drinks then GARY drinks. GARY starts to flap his front feet and begins to fly.)

MAX: Hey – Wait for me!

(MAX flaps his arms and flies high in the air.)

MAX: Wow! I can fly! This is amazing!

(MAX and GARY fly over the Indian jungle and the Russian palace, where the MONKEYS and PRINCE sing about cocktails and peas down on the ground.)

The End.

The Magic Wig

BY ISABELLE KENNEDY-GRIMES

SCENE 1

An old, grumpy, bossy, very well-spoken, woman named MRS. WALLACE walks into MR. WATSON's Wig Store in St. James'.

MRS. WALLACE: Excuse me. I am looking for a grand wig that would win 1st Prize at the Ball at St. James' Hall on the terrace.

SHOP KEEPER: Oh well, you're just in time because there is only one more wig left on the shelf.

MRS. WALLACE: Splendid.

(MRS. WALLACE walks over to the fancy wig and examines it to see if she likes it.)

SHOP KEEPER: So, do you like it?

MRS. WALLACE: Oh, yes. How much is it?

SHOP KEEPER: Oh, that will be £25.

MRS. WALLACE: My goodness. That's a lot of money. Oh well. I'll take it anyway.

(MRS. WALLACE hands the shopkeeper her money and the shop keeper wraps the wig in a paper bag and hands it to MRS. WALLACE.)

SHOP KEEPER: There you go, Madam. Enjoy your Ball.

MRS. WALLACE: Yes.

(MRS. WALLACE walks away without saying thank you.)

SCENE 2

MRS. WALLACE is now outside and walking down Pall Mall towards the Hall at St. James'.

MRS. WALLACE stands outside the terrace of St. James' Hall and slips on the new wig.

MRS. WALLACE immediately turns to stone – still keeping her brain.

MRS. WALLACE: Oh golly. What's happened? I can't move. I feel like I've turned to stone. Oh, I hate this. I will never get to the Ball on time. Oh, no. What did I do wrong to deserve this?

(Two BUILDERS drive by St. James' Hall in their rusty old van. They stop at the lights and see MRS WALLACE.)

BUILDER 1: Ello Darlin'. Nice 'air.

(BUILDER 2 looks at his mate.)

BUILDERS 2: Yeah! For a bird's nest!

(Both BUILDERS start laughing and drive off as the traffic lights change to green again.)

(Curtains close and open again.)

(The BUILDERS who were there earlier drive past again on the way home and see MRS. WALLACE.)

BUILDER 1: Lets check 'er out.

BUILDER 2: Mmm.

(The BUILDERS begin to examine MRS. WALLACE.)

BUILDER 2: Look, Dan, she don't look famous to me and I know every famous statue around.

BUILDER 1: Yeah, but she still might be an antique.

MRS WALLACE: Oh how dare he. I'm not old!

BUILDER 2: Let's take her to a dealer.

BUILDER 1: Ok then.

(The BUILDERS pick up MRS WALLACE.)

MRS WALLACE: Oh, put me down you idiotic men!

(The two BUILDERS dump MRS WALLACE into the back of the van.)

MRS WALLACE: Let me out!

BUILDER 1: I think that we'll make millions and millions of pounds out of her.

BUILDER 2: Yeah, we'll be rich.

(BUILDER 1 starts the engine and drives off.)

BUILDER 2: Eh look. Stop stop. There's the dealers, your going past it.

BUILDER 1: Alright mate, calm down.

(BUILDER 1 parks the van outside the dealers and unloads the statue.)

MRS WALLACE: Oh my goodness. They're taking me to a dealer. What do they think they are doing?

(THE BUILDERS carry the statue over to the DEALER who is standing outside his shop.)

BUILDER 2: Eh mate. Watch the bird's nest. Easy does it.

MRS WALLACE: If you don't mind, this is a very expensive wig.

(The DEALER opens the shop door and looks at the two BUILDERS and the statue. He looks confused.)

DEALER: Hello gentlemen. How can I help you?

MRS WALLACE: Well at least someone can speak proper English around here.

BUILDER 1: 'Er we were just wondering how much this statue of ours is worth.

(The DEALER looks at the statue carefully and looks puzzled.)

DEALER: Umm where did you get her from?

BUILDER 1: Umm we just got 'er from the charity shop down the road.

DEALER: Interesting. How much did you pay for her, if you don't mind me asking?

BUILDER 2: Um umm err.

(*BUILDER 1 looks at BUILDER 2 puzzled.*)

BUILDER 2: Um er I can't remember.

DEALER: Oh well, never mind. Well I have to say I have never seen anything like it before. She certainly looks old.

MRS WALLACE: Old? Old? How dare you. I'm not old.

DEALER: Even so, I am going to say that she is only worth about about ten…

BUILDER 1: Yeah. Ten what? Hundred? Thousand? Million?

DEALER: Umm no. I would say ten pounds, but I wouldn't sell her in my shop.

BUILDER 2: So, not so valuable eh?

MRS WALLACE: How dare you, I am verrrrry valuable. This is a disgrace.

DEALER: No, I'm afraid not. Sorry that I can't be more helpful but I don't sell statues.

BUILDER 1: Come on Dave let's take her to the dump.

MRS WALLACE: THE DUMP! THE DUMP! How dare they take me to such a hideous place. Do they not know I'm a human being?

SCENE 3

The BUILDERS arrive at the dump and open the van.

BUILDER 2: Come on mate. There's a good spot.

(*The BUILDERS carry MRS WALLACE over to the dump and chuck her onto a pile of rubbish.*)

MRS WALLACE: Oh how dare they. What would my mother say? My friends will be worried that I am not at the Hall and they certainly should be. I should be dancing and having fun at the Ball, not lying on a dump. Oh somebody please help me.

(The BUILDERS look at MRS WALLACE.)

BUILDER 1: Bye darling.

BUILDER 2: Hope your eggs hatch alright in that bird's nest of yours.

MRS WALLACE: IDIOTS!

(The BUILDERS drive off laughing.)

BUILDER 1: Shame she weren't worth nothing.

BUILDER 2: Yeah.

(A while later a little girl and her dad arrive at the dump with a van full of rubbish.)

(The little girl spots the statue and is drawn to it.)

LITTLE GIRL: Oh daddy, daddy, daddy look what I've found. An old lady statue.

MRS WALLACE: As I have said before and I will say it again, I am not old!

(The DAD comes over to take a look.)

DAD: Gosh, that's unusual.

LITTLE GIRL: Oh Daddy please can I have her please, please, please, please?

MRS WALLACE: At least somebody wants me but does it have to be a child. I hate children – this is the worst day of my life.

DADDY: Why on earth would you want that old thing?

LITTLE GIRL: Oh, for my party! My friends would love her! I could put her in the garden. Oh please can I have her. Please, please, please?

DAD: Oh I don't know.

(The LITTLE GIRL starts to cry.)

DAD: Oh go on then.

(The LITTLE GIRL puts on a big grin.)

LITTLE GIRL: Oh thank you Daddy! Thank you. Thank you.

DAD: Look I just unloaded a load of rubbish and now I have to put more rubbish back in now.

MRS WALLACE: RUBBISH? I'LL GIVE YOU RUBBISH!

DAD: Come on let's go home, Lucy.

(LUCY's DAD picks up the statue and puts her in his van.)

DAD: I hope your mother won't go ballistic.

LITTLE GIRL: She won't. Anyway, we need a nice statue for the garden and I can make her look pretty for my party.

MRS WALLACE: I'm already pretty!

SCENE 3

LUCY and her FATHER come home with the statue and see LUCY's MOTHER clearing out the garden.

LUCY: Mother! Mother! Look! Look! I've got a statue for the garden.

MUM: Oh, wonderful! Let me see it!

(LUCY's MOTHER comes over and looks at the statue.)

MUM: She looks a bit ugly don't you think?

MRS WALLACE: I'm not ugly. I am very beautiful.

LUCY: No mother. I think that she looks lovely.

MRS WALLACE: Why I'm beginning to feel a little touched by a child and I don't normally like children.

LUCY: Come on Dad. Let's put her in the garden.

(LUCY's DAD walks back in to the house and LUCY and MRS WALLACE are left alone.)

LUCY: I like your hair, do you want to have some glitter in it? I bet you do.

(LUCY goes to get some glitter and sprinkles it all over MRS WALLACE.)

MRS WALLACE: Oh my goodness, I'm beginning to actually love children now.

(Soon LUCY went inside and the wind blew away all the glitter.)

(One morning MRS WALLACE sees a Happy Birthday sign outside in the garden.)

MRS WALLACE: Oh, they even know my birthday date.

(A whole load of kids come rushing outside singing 'Happy Birthday'.)

KIDS: Happy Birthday to you. Happy Birthday to you.

MRS WALLACE: Oh now I love kids.

KIDS: Happy Birthday dear Lucy, Happy Birthday to you!

MRS WALLACE: Hey! My name is not Lucy! Oh well I still like children much better now as they are such cheerful little things.

(In the evening MRS WALLACE felt a little sad.)

MRS WALLACE: Oh how I do wish that I could tell Lucy how much I appreciate her looking after me.

(Curtains close and open again.)

(The next morning MRS WALLACE is pretty cheerful and is realizing that children aren't so bad after all.)

(Suddenly some raindrops begin to fall from the sky and MRS WALLACE begins to change.)

(MRS WALLACE's face begins to turn all beautiful, MRS WALLACE's dress appears in colour and her wig begins to fade as she appears to have a bun. MRS WALLACE is turning into a human again.)

MRS WALLACE: Oh dear it's raining. Wait, I can feel the rain. What's happening? I'm changing!

(Suddenly LUCY comes outside and sees MRS WALLACE as a beautiful, young woman. LUCY looks puzzled.)

LUCY: What did you do to my statue?

MRS WALLACE: Oh I am the statue. The rain must have made me change back into a human. I was on my way to a Ball when I put on my new wig and I turned to stone. Now I would like to thank you for being so kind to me.

LUCY: Oh you're welcome.

(MRS WALLACE and LUCY begin to dance together and the curtains close.)

(Suddenly the curtains open again and all of the characters bow.)

(The show is now finished and the curtains close again.)

The End.

Journey to Food Paradise

BY JOSE LUIS AQUINO-MEJIA

Cast

DOUGHBOB CREAMHEAD

NARRATOR: OLD PRETZEL MAN

PRETZEL MAN

BARON BON CANDY CANE

SCENE 1 EATOPOLIS

NARRATOR: Welcome I'm here to tell you an adventure of an old friend of mine DoughBob CreamHead.

DOUGHBOB: *(Walking along the road.)* Should I go to the news billboard or the café?

NARRATOR: Surprising DoughBob I came along cheerfully.

PRETZELMAN: *(Excited.)* Hiya DoughBob how ya doing?

DOUGHBOB: *(Surprised.)* Oh I'm fine and how's the job finding working out?

PRETZELMAN: It's fine but I'm more interested in you, where ya going?

DOUGHBOB: Actually I was just working out where to go the café or the news billboard, what do you think?

PRETZELMAN: Maybe we should go to the café then the billboard!

DOUGHBOB: That's a brilliant idea let's do those, how funny you bump into a friend then the next thing you know it you're going away with them.

SCENE 2 BOB'S CAFÉ

NARRATOR: There we were in Bob's café, our usual talking place, when suddenly two muscular lollipops with cockney accents burst in.

SHERBERTDEVIL: *(Angry.)* Give us two cuppas on the house or I'll get mi boss to shut you down ASAP.

SWEETSAINTAN: Yeah shut ya down!

SHERBERTDEVIL: Oh be quiet will you or I'll get the boss to fire you.

SHERBERTDEVIL: Mi boss is an eccentric billionaire you know and he's trying to be first to Food Paradise.

BOBMUFFIN: Okay, boys get me two coffees pronto.

WORKERS: Ok boss!

(Whizzing of a kettle and clashing of pots and pans.)

BOBMUFFIN: Here ya go two coffees on the house or as you guys call it cuppas.

(LOLLIPOPS leave.)

DOUGHBOB: *(Annoyed.)* Who do they think they are just because their boss is an eccentric billionaire it doesn't mean they can boss us around like that.

PRETZELMAN: *(Frustrated.)* Let's go I think we've had enough.

SCENE 3: NEWS BILLBOARD

PRETZELMAN: So what's new?

DOUGHBOB: It says the race to food paradise is begun because the humans are trying to destroy food paradise and baron bon candy cane wants to own food paradise.

PRETZELMAN: Isn't food paradise the place that those two lugs was talking about in the café?

DOUGHBOB: Yeah it was, I'm going to get to food paradise before anyone.

PRETZELMAN: Are you out of your mind first you're up with a billionaire, next you're up with humans did you know humans eat us.

DOUGHBOB: I know all that but I'll give it a try besides at last there's gonna be excitement in my life.

PRETZELMAN: I know this is crazy but I'm going with you even if we're going to put ourselves in grave danger a friend's a friend and friends stick together.

DOUGHBOB: *(Happy.)* Thank you so much.

PRETZELMAN: Friends would do anything if it makes their friend happy.

NARRATOR: So we set off to food paradise with nothing in our minds but making it.

SCENE 4 : ETERNAL TOWN

NARRATOR: We were halfway there in a town called eternal city with weeping pastries all around their wrecked city we felt so sorry for them.

PRETZELMAN: What happened here this town is a wreck.

NARRATOR: A beautiful young sausage roll called Sandy stood up and spoke.

SANDY: *(Sad.)* The humans came here and tried to eat all of us but we're eternal and we could grow back from a single crumb. When the humans noticed they wrecked our village instead, we would do anything to have revenge.

DOUGHBOB: *(To PRETZELMAN.)* So this is what humans can do we better be prepared.

PRETZELMAN: *(Out loud.)* Who would like to go with us to Food Paradise with us and claim revenge on the humans!!??

SANDY: I would because I know the way to Food Paradise easily but there are a few bumps in the road.

DOUGHBOB: Okay but we need to know how to be immortal so we can definitely win the race.

SANDY: We shall perform the ritual tomorrow but first we need to rest and before that fix this place up.

NARRATOR: So we fixed the town up and went to sleep. The elder mother performed the rituals on us to be eternal and I DoughBob and Sandy went to win the race to Food Paradise.

SCENE 5: STORM CITY

SANDY: We have to set up camp here, this place is called Storm City it has been deserted for 20 years because of the storms but the houses are stable, you might have Baron bon Candy Cane here though.

(Crash in the city, footsteps are heard, lollipops come in with evil BARON BON CANDY CANE.)

SHERBERTDEVIL: You again what are you guys doing 'ere.

PRETZELMAN: We're here to win the race to Food Paradise.

BARON: *(Interrupting.)* So these were the guys you were talking about. We are definitely going to win this and nobody can stop us, kick them out.

(The three get kicked out and go in another building.)

DOUGHBOB: Let's go to sleep and go straight to Food Paradise even with Baron Bon Candy Cane on our tail they don't know the way.

SCENE 6 FOOD PARADISE

NARRATOR: We made it to food paradise first and we rejoiced so much.

DOUGHBOB: We made it, Sandy I know we knew each other for a few days but now you're one of my best friends and without you guys I wouldn't have ruled Food Paradise in harmony.

NARRATOR: So DoughBob ruled Food Paradise and Sandy and I got together and went back to Eternal Town.

The End.

Mason's Journey

BY NASEEM CHARRAT

(Plot – MASON is a newspaper, not big, not small, just an average newspaper. MASON's days are usually the same…but one day he gets taken out of the bus land and into a real home by some random guy! Will MASON make it back to the bus safely? No one knows.)

SCENE 1

MASON: *(Talking in his head, no one can hear him. Bear in mind he's a newspaper.)* Ahh, another day. Maybe today will be different... perhaps I'll finally have peace and quiet.

(Random GUY steps in.)

GUY: Hey, there's a newspaper! Gotta find out what happened in yesterday's football game... *(Picks up MASON THE NEWSPAPER.)* Ah, today's copy of *The Sun.* I shall keep this.

MASON: Oh great, another day full of crazy-looking people reading me and this guy said he'd keep me. That could mean I go on to live in a big house or it could mean I'm thrown in the rubbish tomorrow. *(There is a moment of silence.)*

Hey, bus has finally stopped. Wait...what? This guy's taking me out, I have a feeling this won't turn out well...

PEOPLE ON BUS: Why's that guy taking that newspaper? No one takes a newspaper. No one takes a newspaper off the bus! Some say it's illegal!

SCENE 2

GUY: Well, I'll be taking this off home, I'll have a good read before breakfast.

MASON: A good read before breakfast... Uh oh, doesn't sound good.

GUY: Is sound coming out of that...? Never mind, it's just a newspaper. Well, it's time I wonder what this week's newspaper will have.

MASON: Better keep quiet, I thought no one could hear me but it seems this guy is different.

GUY: *(Spots another guy giving away free newspapers.)* Now that I think about it, why did I pick up this rotten old thing off the bus? Forget it, now that I have this I may as well keep it.

SCENE 3

GUY: Well, here we are.

MASON: I wonder why that guy's talking to himself. Anyway, my prediction was right. I'm going to live in a house.

GUY: *(Pretending the newspaper can hear him, well, it can but he doesn't know it.)* Well, go find yourself somewhere to rest up and I'll be there in a sec.

MASON: Might as well do what he says... Never mind I have no control even though I can't walk!

(MASON tries to move but fails.)

MASON: If only I could move, I'd become rich and famous! There'd be newspaper articles about Mason the Walking Newspaper!

SCENE 4

GUY: I heard this week's newspaper came out. Oh well, I might as well throw this old one away.

(Takes MASON and throws him into the rubbish.)

MASON: O! Well I'm in the bin now, getting angry won't change anything.

(MASON tries to climb out but it doesn't work.)

MASON: It's no use, I'll never get out of this disgusting place.

(MASON spots a trampoline in the bin.)

MASON: Hey, maybe I can use this...

(He fails at using it.)

MASON: On second thought, I'll move onto Plan B.

The End.

Sports Day Life Saver

BY ANYA DAVIES

SCENE ONE

ABI runs down the stairs excited about sports day. She is wearing her trainers already.

MUM: Slow down it's not the race yet! You don't want to hurt yourself before the race.

ABI: Sorry! I can't believe that you remembered it is sports day this afternoon. *(She shovels her cereal into her mouth.)*

MUM: How could I forget? You have been going on about it all year since last sports day when some girl called Sophie beat you.

ABI: Yes, but we don't talk about that do we? *(She says through gritted teeth.)* Right, have we got any bananas? I need some extra energy.

MUM: *(She passes ABI a banana.)* Oh well it's the taking part that counts. I'll arrive at school to help your class walk to the park.

ABI: Oh no you won't. It's just around the corner, you can meet us there.

MUM: Alright then. I'll meet you there.

ABI: Thank you, at last, some freedom!

MUM: So I'll meet you at the park then.

ABI: Ok. But anyway I've got to get to school before Mr Scott gives me detention. *(She gets her bag on her back and gets ready to leave.)*

MUM: Have a good time at school and don't get too nervous.

ABI: I'll try not to Byee. *(She leaves and shuts the door behind her.)*

SCENE TWO

A school playground. ABI is standing among a group of children chatting and giggling. A teacher walks in.

MR SCOTT: Line up in pairs children. We are leaving for the park soon.

(ABI partners her best friend KATY.)

ABI: Are you nervous?

KATY: Sort of. Are you?

ABI: Yes but I'm excited because I've trained so hard I'm sure to win.

(Standing behind ABI listening to her conversation is her acrh rival SOPHIE – and her partner ANNABEL. SOPHIE pulls a scornful face.)

SOPHIE: Did you hear that Annabel? Abi reckons she is going to win the race! There is no chance of that happening while I'm around. I'll thrash her!

ANNABEL: *(Timidly.)* Yes. I am sure you will win!

ABI: We're here! I'm so nervous. It feels like something bad is going to happen!

KATY: Don't worry! You are so fast at running and even if you don't win it does not matter.

MR SCOTT: Everyone put your bags down. Then we can start.

KATY: Abi, look. There is your mum sitting next to mine in the stands.

(ABI waves to her mum.)

MR SCOTT: The girls' 100 metre sprint will be starting soon. Please make your way to the track if you're running this race.

KATY: Go on Abi. *(She pats her on the back.)*

ABI walks over to the track ready to run.

COMMENTATOR: On your marks, get set, go!

KATY'S MUM: Wow Abi is such a fast runner!

(ABI looks back to the starting line and sees a little boy running towards the main road.)

ABI: *(Whispering under her breath.)* What shall I do? It is Sophie's brother.

ABI runs towards the boy as fast as her lags can carry her.

COMMENTATOR: Runner number three has left the track and is running the wrong way.

(SOPHIE carries on running not seeing that it is her little brother MATTHEW.)

COMMENTATOR: Sophie Armitage wins again!

(ABI comes back on stage carrying SOPHIE's brother.)

SOPHIE: Matthew, what are you doing?

ABI: He was running towards the road so I ran to get him.

SOPHIE: How can I thank you?

COMMENTATOR: Could Sophie please come and receive her medal.

SOPHIE: Thank you.

(SOPHIE steps off the podium.)

SOPHIE: Here. Have my medal.

ABI: Why?

SOPHIE: Firstly you saved my brother's life and secondly you probably ran twice as fast as I did.

ABI: Thank you so much!

The End.

Ella and The Minotaur

BY FLORENCE ADRIAN

ACT I

SCENE I

A shabby bedroom.

Music – 'The Blue Danube'.

ANTOINETTE: *(Evil Stepmother.) Ella.* It's 6 a.m. and you're still in bed!

  (Music stops abruptly.)

ELLA: *(Sleepily.)* What…?

ANTOINETTE: Get up you little ratbag!

ELLA: Oh! Yes, ma'am, sorry ma'am.

ANTOINETTE: That's better.

  (ELLA jumps out of bed and tugs on her shoes. These are worn and patched.)

ELLA: *(Muttering.)* Oh boy. I could 'ave had a lovely stepmother, maybe one who actually *fed* me but no, no I get landed with her.

ANTOINETTE: And don't forget to make breakfast!

SCENE II

(The ugly stepsisters, GEORGINA and URSULA follow ANTOINETTE down the stairs.)

GEORGINA: Where's my breakfast, slug?!

ELLA: Coming, mistress Georgina, coming.

  (Sound of letterbox rattling.)

URSULA: Go and get the post, *worm.*

(Exit ELLA.)

ELLA: *(Handing out the post.)* There's one for you, mistress Georgina, coming.

(Sound of letterbox rattling.)

URSULA: Go and get the post, *worm.*

(Exit ELLA.)

ELLA: *(Handling out the post.)* There's one for you, mistress Georgina, one for you, mistress Ursula…and one for you, ma'am.

(She sees she has her own letter and her eyes widen in shock and hope.)

URSULA: Mummy, Mummy, look, we've been invited to the prince's birthday party! At the nightclub! Oh and he says the girl that he likes most he's going to *marry!*

(Points at herself. GEORGINA sees her, pushes her over and gives a winning smile.)

ANTOINETTE: And what does yours say, Ella? That you've been give the ugliest person of the year award?!

ELLA: Is isn't just mistresses Ursula and Georgina that have been invited, *I have too!*

ANTOINETTE: Give me that! What? It's tomorrow night? Oh, Ella, you can't possibly go tomorrow night!

ELLA: Why?

ANTOINETTE: I mean look at the state of the place! You must spend tomorrow night cleaning. As for now…I need my sausage, egg, bacon, mushroom, tomatoes and…French toast. Come on, chop chop!

SCENE III – A GRAND KITCHEN

GEORGINA: I want my dress sparkly and gold for a golden girl!

URSULA: Mine must be long and glittery, for a glittering girl!

ELLA: They should be ready by about lunchtime tomorrow.

(Enter ANTOINETTE.)

ANTOINETTE: *(Icily.)* And they'd better be. If my darling daughters AREN'T ready by tomorrow lunchtime, you will wish you'd never been born…

SCENE IV – STILL A GRAND KITCHEN

ELLA is helping URSULA and GEORGINA into their dresses. ANTOINETTE watches on with narrowed eyes.

ELLA: There we are. Night clubbing dresses are *(Sighs.)* all ready.

(URSULA rushes over to the mirror.)

URSULA: Wow! I look so fantastic! The Prince is sure to marry me.

GEORGINA: Stop being such a twit, Ursula. The Golden Girl, that's me, will win his hand!

ANTOINETTE: Are you ready, then girls? Come on! *(To Ella.)* And you! I want the floor so shiny that my beautiful girls use it as a mirror.

(They flounce out, leaving ELLA scrubbing and sobbing. Enter FAIRY NIGHTCLUBBER.)

FAIRY NIGHTCLUBBER: You know you *(could)* go if you wanted. It'd be complicated, but I can try.

ELLA: Who *are you*…like my Fairy Godmother?

FAIRY N: Don't call me Fairy *Godmother*, sunshine. It makes me sound so *old!* Ugh. I am the Fairy Nightclubber. The Fairy Godmother takes ladies to the ball, all *that* boring stuff. I am going to take you *(She points a wand at ELLA.)* to the nightclub.

ELLA: But…

FAIRY N: No buts, little lady. Now go get me a courgette and a toad. *(She snaps her fingers and flicks her wand.)*

(Five minutes later.)

ELLA: Here we are.

(FAIRY NIGHTCLUBBER waves her wand and a limousine is where the courgette was, a chauffeur where the toad was.)

ELLA: Thank you so much!

FAIRY N: You'd better get going 'cause my magic will wear off at…

(She checks her watch.) fourteen minutes thirteen point five eight seconds past twelve. You better be on time.

ELLA: I am always on time.

(ELLA jumps in the limousine and drives away. FAIRY NIGHTCLUBBER watches, waves and cries a bit.)

SCENE V – A BUSY NIGHTCLUB

ELLA: *(To the doorman.)* Here's my invite… *(She hands him an envelope.)*

DOORMAN: *(Droning, monotonous voice.)* It's fine. You may come in.

(He lifts a rope and she steps inside. ELLA wanders over to a small table and watches the dancing. A nobleman asks her to dance. ze now see URSULA and GEORGINA sulking in a corner.)

URSULA: We've been here for *two and a half hours and still* nobody has asked me to dance!

GEORGINA: Well, *that's* hardly surprising.

URSULA: What was that?

GEORGINA: You've got as much chance as a hippo has.

URSULA: Shut it you! Hey, look over there, that girl dancing with Lord Sponge looks just like our Ella…

GEORGINA: Can't be. If she left the house, I'll bet you anything that after Mum was done with her she wouldn't be able to sit down for a month.

URSULA: Georgie!

GEORGINA: What?

URSULA: Georgie!

GEORGINA: What?

URSULA: Georgie!

GEORGINA: *What?!*

URSULA: Georgina, look the Prince is coming over *here!*

GEORGINA: You *twit*, Ursula. He's going to ask her to dance, not a weirdo like *you*.

URSULA: Well, thank you very much for your sympathy (!)

(The PRINCE walks over to ELLA and asks her to dance. They step up to the dance floor together.)

GEORGINA: Are my eyes deceiving me or has the Prince just asked that girl that looks like our Ella to dance????!!!!

URSULA: He has. Anyway, I'm going to find Mum. I want to go home *(She stamps her foot.) NOW!!*

SCENE VI

The whole of the nightclub is empty except for the PRINCE and ELLA who are still dancing. ELLA looks at the clock and sees that it is a fourteen past twelve.)

ELLA: Oh, I have to go! *(To the PRINCE.)* I have to go home!

MINOTAUR/PRINCE: *(Evil voice.)* Not today! *(THE MINOTAUR/ PRINCE drags ELLA off stage. She is screaming.)*

End of Act I.

ACT II

SCENE 1

ELLA is in a cage in a dark room. The PRINCE is standing by the cage.

SCENE II

ELLA: Let me *out! (ELLA rattles the bars of her cage.)*

M. PRINCE: Not gonna happen, little lady.

> *(MINOTAUR PRINCE reaches up and tugs at his hair. His mask comes off and his MINOTAUR appearance is revealed.)*

MINOTAUR: Now I have you my plan is almost complete!

ELLA: What?

MINOTAUR: *(Pacing up and down and acting out his story.)* For centuries, my species has been degraded by the humans, until we are so low that we only exist in the Maldives. We want to *expand,* our people want to *breed*, to become one, huge ruling family!!! I was the person who came up with the plan. Me with my brilliant mind and – but that's not the point. We would kidnap the most lovely woman, who the world prized, and hold her captive. We would demand to become rulers of the world. If you refused, we would torture the girl until we got what we wanted.

> *(ELLA smacks her hand on her forehead.)*

ELLA: Why do the bad guys always tell you *their whole* plan *?!*

MINOTAUR: Maybe because they know there's nothing you can do about it. *(ELLA raises her eyebrows and begins fiddling with the door of her cage. The MINOTAUR is getting something out of a cupboard. In the background, ELLA has opened the door to her cage. ELLA walks over to the MINOTAUR and taps him on the shoulder.)*

ELLA: Next time you keep someone prisoner, I'd advise you to maybe, you know, lock the cage?

MINOTAUR: *Real funny.* Now get back in the cage.

(ELLA goes over to the broom cupboard and pulls out the PRINCE.)

ELLA: And now I've got the Prince as well. Looks like your genius plan is going rapidly down hill.

MINOTAUR: If…you…could…just…give…that…here…

(He lunges. ELLA sticks out her leg and he trips. He lies on the ground unconscious.)

ELLA: Hey, are you ok.

PRINCE: You could say.

ELLA: Let's get you home.

SCENE VIII

In the middle of the night. The PRINCE and ELLA are in the kitchen holding mugs of tea and sipping from them.

PRINCE: Thank you, you know, for rescuing me.

ELLA: Oh, it was nothing, really. All in a day's work. So what happened to you? How did you come to be in a broom cupboard?

PRINCE: Oh you know, it was the classic kidnapping. The minotaur crept in, knocked out the guards and sneaked up on me as I was playing chess. He bundled me in a sack and knocked me out. Next thing I knew I was in a dark, gloomy cupboard.

ELLA: Well, after that escapade, I should think you'll be wanting your own warm bed. I'll just go and get a cab…

PRINCE: No! Wait. Is there anything I can do for you?

ELLA: As a matter of fact, there is something that really should be dealt with…

SCENE VIIII

In the palace kitchen. URSULA, GEORGINA and ANTOINETTE are slaving away at the washing up.

URSULA: I could have grown up and been a movie star. But look where I've landed. And all because of that wretched Ella.

GEORGINA: Exactly. I could have been a princess. I could have lived in a mansion with an en-suite jaccuzzi. But no. Look at us, slaving away in a palace for a prince that could have married me.

URSULA: No, if he'd married anybody it would have been me. You had as much chance with him as a skunk.

ANTOINETTE: Girls! Stop bickering and get on with the washing up! I'm doing all the work here!

URSULA: That's what life's all about now, isn't it? Work.

ANTOINETTE: I'm afraid so, girls, I'm afraid so.

The End.

The Origin of Bad Guy Rope

BY TEMIDAYO ABAYOMI-JOSEPH

SCENE 1

NARRATOR: In a lab far, far away…

VIKTOR: *(Speaking to the government.)* Hello gentlemen, welcome. I am Viktor von Bottle. I have come to show you the new generation of ropes, I present to you, the Super Rope!

PRESIDENT: Excuse me, Mr von Bottle, but what does it do?

VIKTOR: Well let's see. It can't be cut, it's ultra-thin, ultra-strong, ultra POWERFUL, has its own life, it can fly with super-speed and can shoot ultra-strong string to tie things.

(General murmuring.)

NARRATOR: Later that night…

(Sound of sirens.)

ASSISTANT 1: Sir, the rope has escaped!

VIKTOR: WHAT?

NARRATOR: As the sirens sounded, the rope ran, not knowing his heritage or his powers …

SCENE 2

NARRATOR: A few days later, after the incident, BAD GUY ROPE woke up in a bin…

ROPE: What's going on? Where am I? Who am I?

NARRATOR: BAD GUY ROPE wandered around til he got to the top of a roof and fell off.

ROPE: Aarrgghh!… Huh, wh –

NARRATOR: BAD GUY ROPE found himself lying on a piece of rope!

ROPE: Wow! Hey, I'm floating.

('Zoom' sound.)

NARRATOR: BAD GUY ROPE found himself zooming through the air.

ROPE: Oh yeah.

SCENE 3

VIKTOR: So he escaped? I guess I'll have to destroy him. You see, there is a special type of mineral… Heh, heh I'll show you!

SCENE 4

NARRATOR: BIG GUY ROPE is flying until he feels his power is gone and falls down from the sky.

ROPE: ARRRGGGH!

MYSTERIOUS VOICE: Well, rope how goes the day?

ROPE: Who are you?

VOICE: I am Viktor von Bottle, respected scientist, your creator and your destroyer.

ROPE: What?

VIKTOR: Yes, I made you, but you will be annihilated! Meet Super Rope Mark II!

(Massive rope stomps onto the scene.)

Try and beat it now!

(ROPE becomes determined and 'game music' comes on.)

GAME 1: Scientist VIKTOR challenges you to a battle.

GAME 2: What will you do? Attack, Items or Run?

GAME 3: BAD GUY ROPE used 'tie'!

GAME 4: VIKTOR used 'stomp'!

(A few minutes later… SUPER ROPE MARK II is destroyed.)

VIKTOR: Urgh, useless thing! Ah, BAD GUY ROPE, anyway see ya! Hy ya!

(Throws smoke bomb but is seen running away.)

NEWS REPORTER: Well, well, well. It looks like there's a superhero here in –

ROPE: No! I am not a superhero, I'm a vigilante and I am BAD GUY ROPE!

(Music: theme to 'Iron Man'.)

The End.

The Emperor's New Fudge

A SHORT PLAY BY LUCAS FERRAR

Cast

Three entrepreneurial schoolboys
(JAMES, CHARLIE, FREDERICK)

FOUR MUMS

SCENE 1

A sweet shop store room. Dusty boxes full of sweets; a cracked window through which only watery light manages to penetrate; a small wooden table laden with chemistry equipment, jars with gaudy powders and bottles of coloured liquid. A chart on the wall shows sweet purchases and sales.

JAMES: That's just great isn't it? No one buys our sweets anymore and we have five hundred jars of super sherbert suckers to get through after Frederick put the decimal point in the wrong place for the order.

CHARLIE: *(Laughing!)* Don't get me started on *that* point. I still can't believe he bought about a million rainbow razzlers just because, apparently, his calculations said they were worth 5,000 rupees each in India.

JAMES: Actually, I think the conversation confusion might have had something to do with the fact that the Year Ones had a sugar rush and did the conga through the staff room.

CHARLIE: *(Tentatively, guiltily.)* Or maybe it has something to do with the four dental implants the Head had to have after she had one of my mega sour sugar-melons.

JAMES: *(Sniggering.)* How do you know that?

CHARLIE: *(Touchingly.)* The Head gave me a very interesting two-hour lecture on it.

JAMES: Hey, you said you went to the Head's office because you beat up the school bully.

CHARLIE: *(Pretending not to have heard JAMES.)* Besides, it's *just* like clueless Frederick to mess up with a basic maths problem…

(Enter FREDERICK.)

FREDERICK: *(Coldly.)* Well, you were the one who refused to help me with my homework, weren't you. And, by the way James, maybe the reason why your sweets don't sell is that they look like frozen sewage, and taste like something out of my toilet.

JAMES: *(Spitefully.)* Maybe so, but at least I wasn't assaulted by the dentist after selling sweets at the school fair.

CHARLIE: Stop bickering you two. Sorry to break it to you but it doesn't matter whose sweets taste like what as we won't be selling any more sweets if we don't come up with something soon.

FREDERICK: Who are you – official peacekeeper or something?

(Despite this they settle down with a look of great concentration on their faces.)

JAMES: *(Smirking.)* Charlie mate, do you always look like you have constipation when you think?

CHARLIE: *(Annoyed.)* Shut up you idiot. Maybe I do have constipation but if so it's in my head.

FREDERICK: Is that a witty but not so witty way of saying you have no…

CHARLIE: *(Positively livid.)* If you say one more thing I'm going to hit you so hard your great grandma's false teeth fall out.

FREDERICK: Okay, okay I get the point, now if you bunch of idiots could poss…

CHARLIE: Oh I give up! You want to surround yourself with lame jokes eh? Well let's see how well you get on without my help, you bunch of lame-brains.

(CHARLIE leaves the room.)

JAMES: So what are we going to do now?

FREDERICK: Raid the school tuck shop and pray for the rest of our lives?

JAMES: Apart from stupid ideas which make me want to punch you in the head.

FREDERICK: Oh, we may have a problem then.

(Silence, apart from the sound of FREDERICK rapping his fingers on the table.)

JAMES: I'm surprised your mum hasn't gone insane yet.

FREDERICK: Oh no, not my mum – she's made of stronger stuff. Now my dad, well he's a different matter.

(Suddenly, CHARLIE enters the room as a run. He knocks into a shelf, which sends books cascading down. A book lands at JAMES's feet with a thud.)

JAMES: *(Picking up a fallen book.)* *(To himself.)* Hmmmm mmm Fairy Tales…that gives me an idea *(Stands for a few moments whilst the idea forms then, to the others.)* …our own, sweet, modern version… *(Shouts.)* Eureka!

FREDERICK: *(Wearily.)* Yeah, you stink too.

JAMES: *(Excitedly.)* No I've got it!

CHARLIE: Well hit me with it then.

(FREDERICK reaches over and punches CHARLIE.)

CHARLIE: *(Puzzled.)* Why the flip did you do that?

FREDERICK: *(Puzzled.)* But you said hit me with it.

CHARLIE: *(Despairingly.)* Oh never mind…

JAMES: *(Brightly.)* Look, our sweets are revolting, disgusting, unpalatable, right?

(Nods and general noises of agreement from others.)

JAMES: Well, that doesn't matter anymore. Just spread the word that the more intelligent you are, the more delicious the sweet tastes. That way, even though it might taste horrible to them, people will buy them so everyone thinks they are intelligent. Da-da.

CHARLIE: *(Astonished.)* That is such a good idea; I don't know whether to be fantastically relieved or insanely jealous.

FREDERICK: Well, let's go start spreading the word.

CHARLIE: Oh my friend, I do not seem to be able to get up.

FREDERICK: *(Sadly.)* Such is the way of life…

JAMES: *(Angrily.)* Well I'm not waiting for anything, you idiots.

(JAMES shoves CHARLIE out the door. FREDERICK tails after.)

SCENE 2

The playground. A group of MUMS are assembled in the playground, which is a strip of concrete with the school in the background. There is a buzz in the air. JAMES is watching from the side.

MUM 1: Have you heard about the new sweet? The one which tastes amazing to intelligent people? My Bertie can't get enough of them!

MUM 2: *(Earnestly.)* Hey, have you heard about Lisa in Year Three? She actually fainted, the sweets tasted so revolting to her. That would explain why she's always languished in the bottom sets.

MUM 3: *(Overhearing annoyed.)* Excuse me, I'm Lisa's mum and I can assure you that she thinks they are absolutely delicious.

MUM 2: *(Boastfully.)* Well my Sophie says they taste like paradise in a wrapper.

MUM 4: *(Pompously.)* Well…well, the sweets are so delicious to my Liam that he says it tastes like ambrosia to the gods.

MUM 1: Huh, when my Bertie had his second sweet, he said it was like having Mozart perform for him.

MUM 3: *(Competitively.)* That's nothing compared to Lisa! After she had her sweet she was ready to conduct Mozart.

MUM 2: That may be but I'll have you know that my daughter could have composed Mozart. Beat that!

MUM 4: After sucking on his third sweet, Liam went on to write a play that won the competition at school.

MUM 3: Is that all? Lisa recently wrote a play that was performed at the local theatre. Voilà!

MUM 1: Well *(Triumphantly.)* my Bertie is having his play performed at the *Royal Court Theatre*.

(JAMES walks towards centre stage.)

JAMES: *(Charmingly.)* Well ladies, it's clear to me that your highly intelligent children have got it all from you.

(He turns to the audience and winks.)

The End.

Baby Sister

BY RUBY DAVID-PIMLOTT

Cast

AMY
A Year Six pupil determined to find her baby
sister, Lily

LILY
Amy's soon-to-be-discovered baby sister

MUM
Amy's mum, now remarried to Amy's dad

STEP DAD
Been married to Amy's mum for 5 years

JESSIE
Amy's BFF

BORIS
Annoying boy in Year Six

MISS UNPAIN
Amy's Year Six teacher

OLD MAN
Cornish fisherman

DAD
Amy's real dad

SCENE 1

Flat in London. A girl's room.

AMY: *(Writing in her diary thinking about what she's writing.)*

Dear Diary,

I've just found the best news ever! I'm not an only child; I have a baby sister, Lily I'm so excited to see her. You know I found out on Twitter. Mum doesn't have one but she went to my stepdad's and found my real dad and...

MUM: Amy your dinner's getting cold!

AMY: COMING! *(Back to thinking.)* I've got a little sister in Cornwall!

MUM: AMY! NOW!

AMY: COMING! *(Back to thinking.)* But I don't know how to get there, anyway bye!

(AMY rushes down the hall to the kitchen where her MUM and STEPDAD are eating their toad in the hole.)

MUM: Where have you been? I thought you had abandoned us then!

AMY: Sorry. *(Sitting down.)*

STEPDAD: And sorry you should be, now eat up your mother's toad in the hole, it's delicious!

AMY: Yer right, it's a Sainsbury's own!

MUM and STEPDAD: Very funny *(Laugh.)* I think we know that Amy!

AMY: *(Starting to eat.)* Well you are right, it is delicious.

MUM: And guess what? Jelly and ice cream for pud! And you know, we made that jelly yesterday!

AMY: I know Mum and I can't wait!

SCENE 2

At School.

AMY: …and I'm going to see her very soon!

JESSIE: (BFF) Wow! You're so lucky you've got a baby sister. I've got two older brothers!

AMY: I know, AND I found her on Twitter!

JESSIE: Really, the internet these days, it's so helpful!

AMY: I know, I don't know what I'd do without it!

BORIS: *(Boy in class.)* So what are you two talking about then?

AMY: Nothin.

JESSIE: Yer, not really anything.

BORIS: Are you telling the truth?

AMY and JESS: Of course!

JESSIE: What do you think we are lying…lying monsters? That's it, monsters!

BORIS: No! You're two weird girls in my class! *(BORIS runs away.)*

AMY and JESS: *(Chasing after him.)* You come here now!

SCENE 3

In Class.

AMY: *(Day dreaming.)*

MISS UNPAIN: Amy what are you doing? Get to your work NOW!

AMY: Sorry Miss Unpain.

MISS UNPAIN: Good, now stop day dreaming.

AMY: I will.

SCENE 4

Back at Home.

AMY: When can I see Lily?

MUM: I don't know.

AMY: Will you let me see her?

MUM: I don't know.

AMY: Please let me see her.

MUM: I'll think about it.

AMY: Please, oh please, oh please.

MUM: I SAID I DON'T KNOW!

AMY: Don't shout at me!

MUM: I can do whatever I want, now don't talk to me like THAT! GO TO YOUR ROOM!

AMY: Fine, I will.

STEPDAD: What's all the commotion about?

AMY: None of your beeswax!

MUM: GO TO YOUR ROOM!

AMY: I'm GOING!

STEPDAD: What happened to your sweet little girl? Eh?

MUM: I don't want to see Lily or her dad, he's dangerous.

SCENE 5

In Amy's Bedroom.

   (AMY writing in her diary thinking about what she is writing.)

   Dear Diary,

I am so angry at Mum. I know she is never going to let me see Lily. And I really want to see her. That is why I'm going to run away. I'm going to Cornwall. Jessie is going next week as it is the summer holidays. They'll take a van because her dad's a musician and has loads of kit. I know I'll be in a big trouble but I am going to hide in the luggage and get to see Lily.

SCENE 6

Next week on the way to Cornwall in the back of the van.

(AMY writing in her diary thinking about what she is writing.)

Dear Diary,

I'm on my way to Cornwall. YIPPEE! Mum is going to be worried out of her guts but who cares. I'm going to get into being trouble but who cares! I'm going to see Lily that's the main thing! Apparently they live in a place called Padstow. Just by the harbour. And guess where Jessie is going to stay? PADSTOW! YIPPEE again!

SCENE 7

In Padstow.

They stop at Tesco's in Padstow to get some shopping for their holiday. Everyone gets out apart from MUM who is listening to the radio. AMY climbs out the back of the van. She starts towards the harbour and bumps into an old man.

OLD MAN: Where are you going in such a hurry?

AMY: I need to find my dad.

OLD MAN: And where's he?

AMY: Well, he's at home and his house is number 9 Lingenbury Street in Padstow, here!

OLD MAN: *(Pointing.)* Well, he lives…down that street then.

AMY: Thank you!

(AMY runs to the street and walks to number 9. She knocks on the door.)

AMY: *(Saying to herself.)* What am I going to say?

DAD: Hello, who are you?

AMY: Is that you Dad?

DAD: You're Amy? I didn't think your mum would let you come.

AMY: She didn't I ran away.

DAD: Oh come in and warm yourself up. I do think we should phone your mother and let her know you're safe.

AMY: Do we have to?

DAD: Yep!

AMY: Mum thinks you're dangerous. You don't look dangerous.

DAD: *(Laughing.)* That was when I was a teenager when I was drunk and took drugs. I'm a married family man now with a new wife and a new baby daughter Lily but I never stopped loving you Amy. Let's ring Mum and tell her you are ok and maybe she will let this be the start of many holidays for you in Cornwall with your baby sister Lily.

AMY: *(Laughing.)* This is a dream come true Dad. Let's phone Mum now. I need to say I'm sorry.

SCENE 8

The next day in DAD's House.

MUM: Oh my beautiful baby, my beautiful baby, you're safe.

DAD: Hi Joy.

MUM: Hi Richard. I can see you've changed your ways. Thanks for looking after Amy. Is this Lily? She is beautiful.

DAD: Yes. Nearly as beautiful as Amy was at this age!

VOICEOVER: Amy and Mum stay for a few weeks. They are lucky because Dad has a guesthouse in Padstow, his new business. This is the start of many happy holidays for Amy and Lily in Padstow together.

The End.

The Delinquent & The Nerd

BY SULTAN ODUKOYA

SCENE1

(DELINQUENT passes everybody in a snazzy type of way. DELINQUENT bumps into NERD.)

TORI THE DELINQUENT: *(Exaggerated.)* What are you doing 4 eyes? You got geek germs all over me, you freak.

(Crowd say 'ooh'.)

JORDAN THE NERD: Sorry Tori. I never knew you were there. I'll stop bothering you now. I was just going to…

TORI: I don't care if you need to go to the swag shop to upgrade your swagger level. But I will forgive you if you take my books to literary class. You're welcome.

SCENE 2

MS DUELL: Here are the teams for the scrap movie. David, you're with Sue; John, you're with Natalie; Andrew, you're with Carleen; Lawrence, you're with Jane; Lee, you're with Julian; Ian, you're with Rachel; Harry, you're with Magaret; And Tori, you're with Jordan.

TORI: Ms Duell, I can't be with the nerd, it just isn't human, zombies don't go with vamp – they hate their undead blood. It's the same with me and nerds.

JORDAN: Yeah, I can't be with this diva.

MS DUELL: Well I'm sorry but it was either this or you had to get an F–, again.

SCENE 3

TORI'S MUM: Come on Tori, we're going to be late!

TORI: Well, excuse me for butting in on your date with the boss!

TORI'S MUM: I will give you double your allowances for a year if you just please promise to be good at Lorna and Jordan's house.

TORI: *(Firm.)* No, he's a nerd.

TORI'S MUM: *(Begging.)* Triple?

TORI: 2 years.

TORI'S MUM: Deal. Touch on it?

(MUM walks off.)

TORI: Just to let you know, to all those Jordans, to have a geek with your name, my apologies.

SCENE 4

TORI: *(Cold.)* So, ready to make a movie? Don't tell ANYONE about my glasses.

JORDAN: Won't spread to a soul, ready to get geek germs all over you?

TORI: *(Sorry.)* Oh my gosh, I'm turning into a nerd, I just need out of the market Gok Wan specs.

JORDAN: *(Questioning.)* Seriousl…

TORI: Zip the lip, if you do, after we do the movie for the day, I'll give you the Tori makeover.

JORDAN: OK. Can I tell you something?

TORI: Spill the beans.

JORDAN: I'm doing this so I can win the movie festival.

TORI: I'm doing this to win Ms Popularity.

JORDAN: If we both win, happy ending, I guess. And what are you reading?

TORI: I am a hiphop girl with a geek so nerdy he can turn into Super Geek.

SCENE 5

JORDAN: What do ya think girls?

(Wait.)

TORI: Magnifique! Ready to change that ricidulous hairstyle?

JORDAN: I guess so.

(Goes to hairstylist and lets him do his work.)

TORI: *(French accent.)* Ooh, excellent!

(JORDAN starts screaming but actually realises his hairstyle is alright.)

JORDAN: Thanks, I guess it's okay.

TORI: You're welks.

JORDAN: I'll drop you home if you like.

TORI: Yeah, I'd like that.

SCENE 6

TORI's best friend.

SAPPHIRE: Who's the cute new kid?

TORI: *(Proud.)* That's Jordan Daniel Jones.

SAPPHIRE: *(Admiring.)* The work of the Tori makeover.

TORI: You're right.

(No. 1 school jock IAN BUTT WALSH walks up to JORDAN looking for a fight.)

SAPPHIRE: Ian's targeted Jordan.

TORI: I know his church priest must hate him with that middle name.

IAN: Yo, four eyes.

JORDAN: Yeah.

(Suspense.)

IAN: Nice job with high tops and all wanna be part of the crew.

JORDAN: I'll stick to my guns, I didn't say no.

IAN: True man.

SCENE 7

BOTH TORI & JORDAN: Guess what?

JORDAN: You first.

TORI: I won Ms Popularity yesterday.

JORDAN: Well I won the Steve Spielberg movie festival.

TORI: Happy ending?

JORDAN: Happy ending.

TORI: Come on, give Momma a squeeze.

(They hug each other.)

TORI: *(Wheezing.)* Oh, geeky smell.

The End.

WWW.OBERONBOOKS.COM

Follow us on www.twitter.com/@oberonbooks
& www.facebook.com/oberonbook